Sis, Who Hurt You?

By Anisha Savery

Copyright

Table of Contents

Introduction
(Note from the author)

The most commonly used phrase is "Daddy Issues" in this book, we are going to talk about building up strong women and facing the lesser talked about "Mommy Issues." The effect of not having an active mother in a young girl's life is just as damaging as having an absent father. Many things factor into a mother-daughter relationship, directly affecting the mother's impact on her child's life.

This book will discuss and go through the painful avenues of abandonment, self-esteem, sexual abuse, and more. This book intends to help encourage healing strained relationships among mothers and daughters and help break the chain of unforgiveness and pain. My prayer is that as you read, any hurt or strained relationships are repaired.

I started this book on the twentieth anniversary of my mother's passing. My mother passed away when I was sixteen, and my mother was my absolute best friend. We had jokes that no one understood but us, and we would have late-night talks while she was doing her dialysis. She would always encourage me to move forward and not be afraid. So, when she passed, I felt betrayed by God because he knew that the one best friend I had was now gone.

My father was not absent. He was very active in my life, but our closeness was not what I had with my mom; I found myself in some intense moments because of my anger at my mother's passing. Looking back, God had a plan for my life. But on the anniversary of my mom's death, I sat on the bed and questioned God. What makes a woman stop wanting to be a mother? What causes problems in young girls? The truth is as young women and mothers, we are all still learning, growing, and healing. I hope that this book will help lead you to a path of healing.

Chapter 1

Who am I?

From the day we are conceived, God knew who we were, what we would look like, the texture of our hair, and our eyes color; he knew us. Today, it is easy for someone to lose the originality of who they genuinely are to be accepted by society. From birth, babies require time, nurturing, and patience, and as the child progresses in life, we begin to understand what cry is for food or what cry is for attention. When they get older, they can use their words to describe what is bothering them or hurting them.

In infancy and childhood, our daughters get a glimpse of themselves in the mirror, also known as her mother's face. If her mother is loving and attuned, the baby is securely attached; she learns that she is loved and lovable. That sense of being lovable—worthy of affection and attention, of being seen and heard—becomes the bedrock on which she builds her earliest sense of self-esteem.

We don't realize that as mothers, our children, especially our daughters, are always watching. They watch how we respond to stress, how we respond to everyday life and mimic what they see.

The daughter of an unloving mother—one who is emotionally distant, withholding, inconsistent, or even hypercritical or cruel—learns different lessons about the world and herself. The underlying problem, of course, is how dependent a human infant is on her mother for nurturance and survival and the circumscribed nature of her world. What results is insecure attachment, characterized as either "ambivalent" (the child doesn't know whether the good mommy or the bad one will show up) or "avoidant" (the daughter wants her mother's love but is afraid of the consequences of seeking it). Ambivalent attachment teaches a child that the world of relationships is unreliable; avoidant attachment sets up a terrible conflict between the child's needs both for her mother's love and protection against her mother's emotional or physical abuse.

Early attachments form our internal templates or mental representations of how relationships work in the world. Without therapy intervention, these mental representations tend to be relatively stable. The critical point is that a daughter's need for her mother's love is a primal driving force. That need does not diminish with unavailability—it coexists with the terrible and damaging understanding that the one person who is supposed to love you without condition does not. The struggle to heal and cope is a mighty one. It affects many, if not all, parts of the self—especially around relationships.

The point of looking at these wounds is not to bemoan them or throw up our hands in despair at the mother-love cards we were dealt but to become conscious and aware of them. Consciousness is the first step in an unloved daughter's healing.

"*There was never a time after my mom passed that I did not think about her, her words of encouragement, the warmth of her hugs, the genuine spirit that she had about her. I would often sit and admire her silent resilience, even if something was bothering her, she never showed it on her face.*" Women are supposed to be unconditionally loving and nurtures of the earth. We are "allowed" to be sensitive but not emotional. I can remember growing up and being told that " no matter how you feel, sick, angry, etc. never to let it show." Even crying was a sign of weakness. I believe that the same people that say "don't cry" may not have dealt with a traumatic situation or are still trying to heal from a traumatic situation.

I moved out of my parent's house at the age of eighteen, but when they put my mother's casket in the ground, a piece of me went with her. Angry, upset, and afraid, I naturally mastered the art of hiding my feelings. I had become detached and not interested in personal relationships; instead of going out with friends, I chose a life of avoidance. Having Mommy issues affects people in many ways; when my mother passed, I decided avoidance.

Suppressed emotions

Suppressing emotions is merely denying these emotions exist. Some people would rather pretend they are not angry or are fearful of not being able to express themselves in a healthy way. Not acknowledging feelings is another way to "cope" with reality.

As mothers, we also help provide our children with a solid sense of awareness. Those children who do not have a stable connection with their mother will also experience something called "False self" or "False sense" of who they are. All children want to be loved, accepted, and made to feel wanted. Sometimes so much so that they lose interest in things that they love and trade them for things that the parent they are seeking affirmations from will see and approve of them. These kinds of behaviors will also impact how we interact with others on friendship levels and romantic levels.

Understanding and knowing who we are will help us open up to others in a healthy way. It will give us a better and more realistic way of handling our emotions and feelings and allows us to have a better understanding of those around us.

Journal

Chapter 2
How We Relate

People go through life wanting to experience love, the gold sweeter than honey love. The first part of love is experienced in our childhood. This type of bond or love comes from a mother to a child that will directly impact the child's ability to love and accept love as an adult. These days, when young girls have babies at a young age, I take it as a sign that they wanted or needed to experience love somewhere along the way. Maybe they were a middle child, and that thought their parents loved the youngest child more. From babies to adults, one thing that people want to experience is love. When people haven't experienced it in their childhood, they may find themselves in unhealthy relationships even as adults.

As we go through life looking for real love and attention, many confuse infatuation with love. An infatuation *is* an intense but short-lived passion or admiration for someone or something.

However, circumstances will teach the child to learn what elements go into love based on their examples; they become adults who seek out relationships based on infatuation. They seek relationships based on what they can get out of the relationship instead of one based on the other person. This leaves them open to being easily manipulated into staying with someone because of the situations in the relationship, not because it is somewhere they genuinely want to be. Any relationship formed out of insecurity is built on a lie. Which is what infatuation is; you are falling for a person you believe they can be and not who they are. The level of love we receive as a child is the building block of how we will allow others to love us and treat us. Listed below are some other types of relationships that can occur due to either a lack of love from our maternal mirror or a maternal mirror that is overbearing.

Abusive relationships

Abuse is not always a physical thing; abuse comes in many forms. Emotional abuse is where one party makes the other believe that no one else could or would ever love them again.

Mental abuse

It's when almost daily, a person is fed lies or manipulated into believing they have to be with the other party for security, love, and attention. These relationships are never okay. If you or someone you know in an abusive relationship encourage them to talk, most abuse victims are not as trusting at first, but once they open up, be the support they need to leave that relationship.

Codependent relationships

A codependent relationship is when a person is physically or psychologically addicted to another person, and the other person is psychologically dependent on them in an unhealthy way. People may feel they have to do things out of the ordinary to keep each other's love and attention.

Independent relationships

To the world, you are a power couple, but you are two people who together can't, won't, or don't know how or are not willing to compromise and sacrifice for the relationship. In this kind of relationship, love is not a priority.

Dominating relationships

There is a demanding presence in these relationships, one person will set all the rules, and you will be required to follow them. And the fact that you are under this "spell" will be clear to friends and family but unnoticeable to you.

The rebound relationship

At some point and time, we fall into this relationship due to our own selfish needs. This relationship rarely works out because it is built on the fear of facing the reality of your recent breakup.

Toxic relationship

This relationship is one in which you and your partner have an extreme attraction to one another but have such drastically different morals, opinions, or integrity that all you do is fight. This relationship is the most exhausting relationship you will experience. There are those relationships that are just for fun; you may enjoy sex with the person, but emotionally you're not too invested; this is just a great distraction.

When you chose to enter into a relationship, there isn't a real way of telling how it will go, but each relationship is a lesson. My suggestion is to learn from it and use the knowledge to make you better.

Journal

Chapter 3

You are Worth the Wait

"Every woman that finally figured out her worth has picked up her suitcases of pride and boarded a flight to freedom, which landed in the valley of change."

— Shannon L. Alder

There are many reasons why women allow themselves to be in a relationship, many have a fear of being alone, and many are dealing with abandonment issues, and some don't know what their worth is. It's been noted as women, we date or choose a potential mate at the level where our self-esteem is, so if a woman has low self-esteem, then the man she dates will find it easier to manipulate and use her and get away with it. When a woman has high self-esteem, they do things differently. Confident women set healthy boundaries.

Healthy personal boundaries and high self-esteem seem to go hand in hand. Having strong boundaries means you can prioritize your needs and emotions and not take responsibility for someone else's needs and feelings. Confident women are not guilted into doing things they don't want to do to keep a man happy or interested. They act in accordance with who they are and what they believe. Confident women trust themselves and their decisions; having high self-esteem is a key component to making the right decision. People with low self-esteem don't trust their judgment, don't trust their gut instincts, and are afraid of being wrong. Which also leads to a life full of anxiety and mistrust.

"If I could leave a note to my younger self, I think it would say… Anisha though the road ahead may get rough, and even though those you love may distance themselves from you, don't lose faith, always believe in yourself and keep fighting.

"After the loss of my mother, I hit a serious spiral, I was depressed, I was angry, and I was alone (or so I felt), that one traumatic experience let my whole guard down, I wound up dating someone who instead of encouraging me to do better and keep up with going to school and finish with my nursing degree he began to get very abusive emotionally and physically.

Although other people could see that the relationship I was in was toxic and unhealthy, I did not see it the same way. Because of my depression and low self-esteem, I remained in the relationship not because I was happy there, but because, at the time, that's what I felt was what I could get. As a result of that relationship, I always sought reassurance in my work life, in my family. After that relationship ended, I realized that I didn't need someone to tell me they loved me constantly; it became something I just knew for myself."

Unfortunately, there are a lot of women who are putting up and dealing with men who are playing with their emotions; they allow the men to make false promises and believe them, then when the guy fails to make good on his promises, we get upset. Getting into a relationship just to say we are in one can lead to a pattern of several bad choices. Ones that one day we may look back and think to ourselves, "I can't believe I gave them a chance or chances." In order to grow, we must be willing first, to be honest with ourselves, second, to be open and willing to change, not to benefit anyone else other than ourselves. Reliance on others can be healthy and affirming. The problem is that as children, we weren't always taught how to balance self-reliance with healthy interdependence.

Being self-reliant can serve us well as adolescents and single adults as we strive to achieve goals and a sense of identity. For instance, "*I was raised in a family where my parents were separated and learned to be independent at a young age, which helped me have great work ethics and succeed in school. But as an adult, developing intimate relationships had been a challenge because it was not always easy for me to draw the line between being independent and relying upon my partner for emotional support.*"

> **Visualize yourself** in an honest and open relationship and work toward allowing yourself to be more vulnerable with your partner — a critical aspect of intimacy.

> **Remind yourself** daily that it's healthy to accept help from others, and it is a sign of strength rather than weakness. This might also apply to your work setting.

Dependence is often seen as a dirty word in our culture. It conjures up images of weakness and insecurity. In actuality, being vulnerable and asking for help when needed, does two things. It shows you are willing to learn to grow and makes your partner feel wanted and needed.

Journal

Chapter 4
Personalities and traits.

How we are raised and nurtured by our maternal mirror also shows how we deal with life situations such as love, work, friendships, and casual meetings. There are several different attitudes that we as people carry, and we adjust them according to our social situation. When children are properly loved and nurtured, they are likely to respond positively to others.

A child with a mother who is not as attentive, or caring is expected to deal with emotional trauma and scars that affect them personally and professionally. Some may experience a strong lack of trust. Lack of trust as a child translates to "How do I know you have my best interest in mind?" "How do I know you won't hurt me?" If not given the proper validation and attention, that same lack of trust then translates over into adulthood as whomever they encounter has a hidden agenda or a plan that may cause them to be taken advantage of.

Lack of trust in an adult; in theory, everyone is suspicious; everyone has an agenda, everyone is out to get them, a slight similarity to schizophrenia. Difficulties setting boundaries is another trait. If a child has a detached mother, they will resort to "people pleasing" to gain favor with the disconnected mother. The reason being they are starved for attention. They desire the love and attachment to their mother by any means necessary.

How this translates into adulthood is a number of unloved daughters report problems with maintaining close female friendships, which are complicated due to issues of trust ("How do I know she's really my friend?"), not being able to say 'no' ("Somehow, I always end up being a doormat, doing too much, and I get used or disappointed in the end"), or wanting a relationship so intense that the other person backs off. Insecurely attached daughters often end up creating scenarios that are more like the "Goldilocks and Three Bears" story than not—never quite right but, somehow, either too "hot" or too "cold." Romantic relationships helpfully further divide those who are avoidantly attached into two categories— "fearful" and "dismissive." Both share the same avoidance of intimacy but for different reasons.

The "fearful" actively seek close relationships but are afraid of intimacy on all levels; they are intensely vulnerable and tend to be clingy and dependent. The "dismissive" is armored and detached; defensively, their avoidance is more straightforward. Alas, both types cannot get the emotional connection that could move them closer to healing. Children who have mothers that only focus on their flaws have a hard time seeing themselves accurately. These distortions in how we see ourselves may extend into every domain, including our looks. Other daughters report feeling surprised when they succeed at something and being hesitant to try something new to reduce the possibility of failure. This is not just a question of low self-esteem but something more profound.

"I've heard mothers tell their daughters, "you would be pretty if your hair wasn't so nappy" or "you're pretty to be fat," and to hear these things catches you off guard. My mother would have never said such things to me, and she did not encourage me to

love myself. But I see its toll on women in adulthood where they feel like to be pretty or accepted, and they must wear the latest fashion, the longest weaves, and fake nails. The way we think about ourselves comes from our maternal mirrors and her love for us." Lacking confidence or feeling fearful sometimes puts the unloved daughter in a defensive crouch. She avoids getting hurt by a bad connection rather than being motivated to find a stable and loving one.

On the surface, these women may act as though they want to be in a relationship, but on a deeper, less conscious level, avoidance is their motivator. The work of Hazan, Shaver, and Bartholomew bears this out. Unfortunately, avoidance—whether fear, mistrust or something else triggers it—actively prevents the unloved daughter from finding the kind of loving and supportive relationships she's always sought. Alas, we tend to be drawn to what we know—those situations which, while they make us unhappy in the end, are nonetheless "comfortable" because they are familiar to us. While securely attached individuals tend to go out into the world, seeking people with similar histories of attachment. Unluckily, so do the ambivalently and avoidantly attached. Sometimes this has the effect of unwittingly replicating the maternal relationship.

Many women go through life not talking about or expressing what they endured in their childhood, so instead of healing, they hold up and store feelings of anger and disappointment and, in turn, pass the same damaging and toxic traits onto their children. The mother's poisonous ways become the unhealthy ways the children learn, and it follows them into adulthood.

Journal

Chapter 5

Past, Present, Future

The way a mother parents or fills the role of a mother is based on her own experiences. As life happens, we mimic what we see and value what we are taught. The most unfortunate part of this is that we go through things that can leave scars way beyond the physical as young women.

Emotional scars may take days, weeks, or years to heal if they ever do. A young woman who experiences a disconnection with her mother will carry on the burden. Her mother may not have been close to her mother; therefore, we have generations of the distance between mothers and daughters. It's easy for people who may not have experienced this to say, "why cause the same pain? Why not provide a different experience?"

Unfortunately, it's not that easy. Why? Because the young woman may not have appropriately dealt with the abandonment of her mother. Therefore, when she gives birth to a child, it's hard for her to share something she never experienced. So, the real question is, who suffers more? The child brought into the world searching solely to be loved and accepted, or the mother seeking approval from her mother? Both suffer, and both go through the pain of not ever feeling good enough or pretty enough and feeling rejected. All things that follow them into adulthood and have effects on them in relationships.

Children of mothers who were disengaged from them suffer an emotional wound that, in many cases, will never heal, even when they seem as though nothing is wrong. It will still be a lingering thought in their minds as to why they weren't "wanted." When children experience this, they suffer from depression and anxiety. In relationships, they tend to be "clingy" to their friends and or their partners. They are "clingy" because being close also provides constant reassurance that they are part of something and that they are not alone.

These children may also exhibit controlling behavior because of the fear of the unknown. These feelings persist as long as the child is in "control" they have power and are comfortable in their situations. However, if a situation comes up that they can't control, they go through unbalanced behavior, which can be unpredictable. Another feeling is anger; children wear anger like a badge of honor. There are two types of anger direct and misdirected.

an·ger/ˈaNGgər
Noun. A strong feeling of annoyance, displeasure, or hostility.

Misdirected anger occurs out of emotion, out of panic, and or anxiety, meaning that it is directed towards something or someone else that has nothing to do with the actual conflict.

Direct anger is when you face your source or point of anger with uncontrollable rage and recklessness.

Many people go through life clinging to direct or indirect anger and hostility simply because they have not found the healing method that is right for them. Without healing from the emotional trauma and anger, these women/ children will also have difficulty getting close enough to someone for fear of the unknown. Most go from relationship to relationship looking for wholeness and happiness but will turn up empty-handed.

Not everyone who endures a traumatic experience is scarred by it; the human psyche has a tremendous capacity for recovery and even growth. Recovering from a traumatic experience requires that painful emotions be thoroughly processed.

Traumatic feelings cannot be repressed or forgotten. If they are not dealt with directly, the distressing feelings and troubling events repeatedly replay in the woman's mind during a lifetime, creating a condition known as post-traumatic stress disorder. In the next few paragraphs, we will discuss the cycles of trauma and how they represent themselves.

Stage One: Circuit-breaking

If you overload an electrical system with too much energy and too much stimulation, the circuit breaker activates and shuts everything down. The human nervous system is also an electrical system, and when it is overloaded with too much stimulation and too much danger, as in trauma, it again shuts down to just basics. People describe it as feeling numb, in shock, or dead inside.

The juice turns off. Intellectually, you lose from 50 to 90 percent of brain capacity, which is why you should never make a decision when you're "in the trauma zone." Emotionally you don't feel anything. Spiritually you're disconnected, you have a spiritual crisis, or it doesn't mean anything to you at all.

Physically all your systems shut down, and you run on basics. What is so intriguing is that physical symptoms that were previously prominent often disappear during this time. Back pain, migraines, arthritis, even acne often clear up. Then, when recovery from trauma is complete, the physical symptoms return.

Stage Two: Return of Feelings

Most people have not experienced so much primary trauma that they must see a professional counselor; they can work through their feelings by working with the closest people in their lives. They do it by telling their story—a hundred times. They need to talk, recount the gory details. It is allowing them to begin to dispel the feelings of distress attached to their memories.

The more that feelings can be encouraged, the better. The more you feel, the more you heal. When our psychological system starts to recover and heal, it can handle a bit more stimulation. The human system is destined to try to recover from traumatic situations. The expression of feelings can take many forms. It may be easier for most people to talk, but others may need to write or draw. However, they tell their stories; the rest of us have an obligation to listen.

There are four broad patterns of expression of feelings that people employ in response to a crisis. Some people consistently maintain one style; others exhibit all four styles at different times. It is essential to recognize which type of emotional expression is characteristic of your response and your loved ones' patterns. Each one demands a different approach.

Stage Three: Constructive Action

People need to take action and make a difference even in the smallest ways. Taking action restores a sense of control and directly counteracts the feeling of power-lessness that identifies the mark of trauma. Traumatic experiences are broken bones of the soul. If you engage in the process of recovery, you get stronger. If you don't, the bones remain porous, with permanent holes inside, and you are considerably weaker. In this stage of recovery, you reintegrate yourself and your values in a new way. You incorporate meaning in your life. You integrate deeper and more authentic ways of communicating

Journal

Chapter 6

Exercising Patience

Children that have suffered from the loss of a parent or an abandonment of a parent seem to be in a rush to find a relationship that will fulfill them. Which, the majority of the time leads them to relationships that can be toxic. When these children are this vulnerable, they go looking for something that will make them feel complete, instead of looking inside and healing.

Healing from the inside out is so critical that it allows us to know who we are and what our boundaries are and what we will and won't accept from a relationship. There are many different types of relationships that people enter and find themselves" trapped." We will go through these and discuss each relationship type as well as any dangers associated with them.

Emotionally filling relationships- These relationships make the individuals feel safe and secure; they appeal to the idea of being "Perfect"; they appeal to the idea of belonging. The downside to this relationship is that once the "honeymoon" phase is over, the emotions change, and the relationship ends. One individual will take advantage of the other's need to belong, that the relationship turns emotionally abusive.

Physically filling Relationships- have you ever seen those couples that look great in public, but there is still a sort of disconnect between them? Those relationships are meant for social media and the public. These relationships can be deceiving because they look perfect, and behind closed doors, we have no idea what's going on. These relationships can also lead to physical abuse. If one of the Individuals wants to leave, the other may become controlling and use physical violence to influence the other to stay.

Infatuation Relationship- These are the relationships where people feel like they found love at first sight. They thrive purely on passion and intimacy with no sign of commitment or longevity.

Fatuous Relationship- These relationships are based on a great relationship's appearance, but there is no substance behind it. This relationship thrives off passion but not intimacy, and with that, when the passion dies, the relationship will die out too.

Romantic Love- This type of relationship, in the beginning, shows signs of being giddy and being so in love, and it has a strong passion and commitment. It's almost reminiscent of a romance novel. It has the potential to be a long-lasting relationship.

Psychologist Robert J Sternberg released his **Triangular Theory of Love in 1985.** Based on his psychological research at Yale University, He used this theory to define different levels of interpersonal relationships and illustrate how these can combine to form the seven types of the thing we call love.

The three components of love interact with each other: For example, greater intimacy may lead to greater passion or commitment, just as greater responsibility may lead to greater intimacy, or with lesser likelihood, greater passion. In general, then, the components are separable but interact with each other.

Although all three components are essential parts of loving relationships, their importance may differ from one relationship to another or over time within a given relationship. Indeed, different kinds of love can be generated by limiting cases of different combinations of the components.

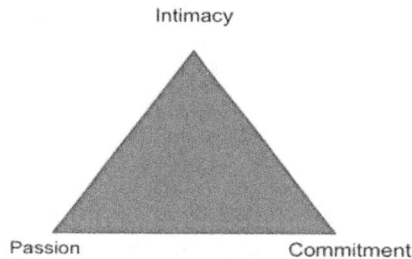

Intimacy

Passion   Commitment

When it comes to love and relationships, it's important to take your time and not rush. It's even more important to know yourself. If not, it can land you in one of the other relationships mentioned; if you are in a relationship, it's okay to set boundaries and determine what is best for both of you.

Robert J Sternberg, Yale University. A Triangular Theory of Love. From Psychological Review,1986, Vol.93, No. 2,119-135. Found at http://pzacad.pitzer.edu/~dmoore/psych199/1986_sternberg_trianglelove.pdf 2 Study.com: Sternberg's Triangular Theory of Love: Definition, Examples & Predictions.

Journal

Chapter 7

The stages of Abandonment

The stages of abandonment align closely with the stages of grief. These stages occur because a person is not ready to understand or agree with a traumatic situation logically. It is these stages that they go through and may be labeled as "troubled." We see children process the stages of abandonment when displaced or when living with a stable parent. There are many emotions that the child goes through. If the child does not resolve anger and depression, they grow and continue into adulthood. The stages of abandonment that children go through may cause them to be labeled as "troubled." This chapter will discuss the stages and how it affects a child and their natural environment or a new living situation.

Denial - is the belief that there is nothing abnormal about the relationship. It is seen through "rose-colored glasses" the situation is only temporary, but it could be very permanent. A child experiencing denial will lash out at authority figures (stepparent foster parent, etc.) in strong hopes that their parent will return. Not all lashing out is aggressive; some can be passive-aggressive and subtle. The child may assume and fear that loving the person standing in the gap, whether a stepparent or family member, may be seen as disloyalty to their absent mother. If a child is going through grief counseling, you may hear the child refer to the missing parent as just being "asleep" that they will see them the following day, when the parent is gone for a lifetime. In our adult lives, denial has different ways of appearing. Some will become "the life of the party," the fun person hiding who they are and what they are genuinely feeling because to see others having fun is a way for them to fill the void of being abandoned.

Depression- this is when the child feels more of the breaking process. The child feels the pull of anxiety and being rejected and may carry around resentment because they could not express anger safely. The child may think that if they continue bad habits like lying, stealing, and lashing out, their mother/ father will want them back. The next best thing is to resent the other parent. As logical as it may seem to a child, we as adults know that will not be the outcome. We tend to carry some of the same anger and rage around and become more like a ticking time bomb. Resentment sets in after anger. It transfers into other things, like self-medicating by being promiscuous, substance abuse, or a history of violence and short-lived relationships. The reason being some feeling of love is better than feeling the empty void and unanswered question of why they were not wanted as a child. Studies have shown that a woman who has always had her mother's influence and a close bond is less likely to be promiscuous than those who have an estranged relationship with their mother.

Acceptance – this is the last stage of abandonment and the beginning of the healing phase. Realizing where you are in a situation and deciding to make the best of it. I wish this were an easy stage to get to; however, it is not. Before people can reach the acceptance stage, the child/adult goes through to get there. These people often have low self-esteem, and they feel they always must prove themselves to others for them to be accepted. This behavior leads to "people pleasing" it is essential for them to that they are liked and want to feel included. If their actions do not lead to the outcome they want, anxiety is front and center. It is another factor people face when seeking acceptance. The reason being most people have been damaged because of a shaky foundation. They automatically assume the worst or have it made up in their mind that they won't be accepted. As the child evolves and with the proper love and support, you will see changes in their mood and behavior. They will no longer feel the need to lie or steal or be aggressive. As adults, when we choose to heal, the same happens as well. The way we think and react in different ways also changes. We start acting out or become irrational, we then develop rational and well thought out plans, and our actions match accordingly. Reaching the stages of acceptance is so important because it is a stage that speaks of mental and emotional growth. It also leads to a chosen path of healing instead of staying in a bad situation.

Holding on to grudges and not letting go of the past can wear on us physically. We can develop health issues by not releasing that which is bothering us mentally. So choosing to heal and letting go helps us inside and out. When we do not choose the path to healing, we will continually find ourselves going through situation after situation until we decide to change. When we self-medicate by using drugs, alcohol, or sex, we remain in a mind-altered state we don't think clearly, which ultimately lands us in a place of confusion and will do more harm than good. If you ever decide to question why you are attracting certain people. You may want to do some introspection to see if you have chosen the healing path or have chosen the path to self-medicate. The answer to what path we chose will be in our actions.

Journal

Chapter 8
The Flawed Mirror

Have you ever seen a mother-daughter duo that is extremely close? They are almost like best friends. My mother was my best friend. We were so close that we could practically finish each other's sentences; we had our inside jokes. She taught me how to cook and do laundry, and life was fun because I was with my best friend. When my mother passed, a big piece of my heart was missing. And I suffered for a while with anger and depression, I tried everything to fill the void of my mother, alcohol, drugs, sex, but nothing was healing that void; instead, it was causing me more harm than good. So I sought healing, which was accepting that yes, life is different, but I had reason to celebrate my mother's life because she was there every moment in my life. So over time, I learned to celebrate my mother's life, who she was, and our friendship.

Fast forward to now, I have a daughter. We, too, are close, and we laugh together; we have our private jokes, just like my mother and me. Saying that to say as mothers, we learn a parenting style from what it is we witness from our mothers. Our strengths, weaknesses, and characteristics all come from what we learn by spending time with our mothers. Unfortunately, not all mother-daughter relationships are healthy. Some mothers use different techniques that stunt their daughters' development instead of encouraging growth. Their daughters go out into the world, sheltered, scared, and naive, which can land their daughters in difficult situations. Have you ever seen a mother-daughter fractured relationship where the mother and daughter aren't close and have little to no relationship? There are different types of mothering styles that either impact the relationship in a way it will grow or in a way that causes it to be fractured.

Narcissistic Mother - The Narcissistic mother is generally self-absorbed; her thoughts and feelings are more important, and her child's needs are insignificant to hers. She makes it easy to neglect or forget about the needs of her children. She terrorizes her child; for all abusers, fear is a powerful means of controlling the victim. Narcissistic mothers use it ruthlessly to train their children.

Authoritarian Mother - This mother is focused on the discipline and authority side. She may believe children should be seen and not heard and have little to no regard for their thoughts or feelings. This mother type has coined the saying, "Because I said so." they limit the child's involvement in problems that weakens their ability to solve problems in the future. Instead, these children grow up to be people-pleasers and will shy away from conflict, and they are at greater risk of low self-esteem due to not feeling valued as a child.

Authoritative Mother - Not to be confused with the Authoritarian Mother, this mother sits down with her children in a non-aggressive manner and explains her actions. These mothers generally have a great relationship with their children. They can talk openly and respectfully about their thoughts and feelings without allowing the kids to believe they are in control of the house. These children grow up with great self-esteem, are confident in themselves, and are comfortable being vocal. Because at home, their feelings and thoughts were validated and heard. Children that have an Authoritative mother tend to be successful and have good decision-making skills.

"Fun" or Permissive Mother – This label has been given to mothers by society and social media and is sometimes considered normal. It is not okay anymore to be the parent that believes in discipline and teaching kids how to respect elders. This mother will set rules and not be strict on the kids to adhere to them; this type of mother is not taken seriously by her children and, the majority of the time, disrespected. The children are not likely to receive any punishments for any wrongdoing. These kids grow up misguided and feeling like they can't talk to their mother about anything because the connection is not there. These children suffer from greater health risks; for example, if their mother isn't paying attention, they may eat junk food rather than regular food. These kids also tend to struggle more in school because they aren't being monitored. These kids are at greater risk because they haven't learned what discipline is; they haven't learned what structure is, affecting them even into adulthood. As a kid, I used to believe my mother had eyes in the back of her head because if I was out with my friends and did something wrong, she knew, but that was the bridge that I needed to be able to have a relationship with her to where nothing was off subject. My mother was fun, but she also had rules that I had to adhere to, and even with my kids, they know that whatever they want to talk about, I'm here to listen and advise them, and even if they don't like what I have to say they know to be respectful.

Uninvolved Mother - The last parenting style is one that hurts my heart the most, and it's the most painful to watch a child go through. It is precisely how it sounds; this mother is not involved with her child at all. This parent rarely knows who her child is with and what they are doing; they rarely ask about schoolwork. Before we go judging, there are some causes, not excuses, behind this behavior. We should consider their mothers' mental health issues. There may be a drug or alcohol-related issue causing the disconnect between her and the child, perhaps even abuse. I've seen these children come out as adults in two different ways. Statistics say that this type of child will suffer from depression, anxiety and perform poorly in school. However, I have also seen people with this type of mother become successful just to show their mother "look what you missed out on"

It's impossible to categorize each mother, we all differ, and all have different traits. What I would like to encourage as a mother is to keep communication lines open with our children. As mothers or soon to be mothers, we have a story and have a past, one we learned from. I would encourage that we use our stories not to scare our children but to let them know the possibilities of what lies out in the real world and let them know they are valued and loved despite our flaws or our mother's flaws. We can break cycles and give our children the life they deserve.

Journal

Chapter 9
What's in Your DNA

Children are known for mimicking what they see and absorb from all of their surroundings. The most influential time of a child's life is from two to about ten years of age. In-between absorbing what they hear and feel, children also start developing attitudes and personalities based on their foundation.

I spoke with a close friend of mine, and she shared her store with me, which was undoubtedly essential to her and her journey. She talked to me about how her lack of attention and love from her mother lead to her journey of addiction, pain, and failed relationships.

She told me that her mother told her things like "she would be much prettier if she were not overweight" when she was a child. She told me that if her mother wasn't poking fun at her, she would yell at her for things that weren't her fault. As a child, she witnessed her mother being drunk; she saw her mother with multiple men. She watched her mother be abused and treated poorly, only to have the man come back. I remember her telling me that "if my mother would have shown me love and kindness and not what I saw, maybe I would not have experienced my trauma."

She experienced the "trickle-down effect" because her mother was being treated poorly in relationships, allowing destructive behaviors in those same relationships. In return, she would receive the same treatment due to her mother's frustration.

As a result of what my friend saw as a child, she instinctively did the same actions in her adult life and those relationships. She loved guys for all the wrong reasons. She allowed herself to be treated poorly, all for the sake of wanting to witness love, true love. Her life became a vicious circle. One day she decided, "I need to love me in order to get better, not drugs." she chose to find a path to healing without destructive behaviors.

Every mother has a backstory; it's a behind-the-scenes look at the life they led before we were born, and some of our mothers were domestic violence survivors, they are addiction survivors, but not a lot of women will tell their kids their back story. It's important to understand the development of the women who gave us life because we know the generational patterns we might be up against.

It also teaches us the area where we are stronger and where we are weak and need help. It gives us a better understanding of who we truly are. We are not our past, nor are we our circumstances. What defines who we are is based on how we handle circumstances.

You will find that you can muster up strength in the most challenging times, and in healing, we build character. Overall, we have to remember that we do not have to remain broken.

One of my favorite stories of strength can be found in the Bible. The woman with the Alabaster box. The box was beautiful and undoubtedly expensive. The oil on the inside was not the standard Kroger Brand oil, but it was the most delicate blend of oil, but she broke it to wash the feet of Jesus.

Matthew 26:7-13

[7] There came unto him a woman having an alabaster box of very precious ointment, and poured it on his head, as he sat at meat.

[8] But when his disciples saw it, they had indignation, saying, To what purpose is this waste?

[9] For this ointment might have been sold for much and given to the poor.

[10] When Jesus understood it, he said unto them, Why trouble ye the woman? For she hath wrought a good work upon me.

[11] For ye have the poor always with you, but me ye have not always.

[12] For in that she hath poured this ointment on my body, she did it for my burial.

[13] Verily I say unto you, Wheresoever this gospel shall be preached in the whole world, there shall also this, that this woman hath done, be told for a memorial of her.

If we take a moment to imagine, we are the box, and we must be broken to get the good oil. If not, we would be basic.

My breaking point was the day my mother passed. My mother was my best friend, my everything. When I lost her, I lost myself and everything I believed in. At sixteen, I needed my mother; I needed her to influence her guidance.

After her passing, I carried the guilt that maybe it was my fault she was gone. I was told that "if my mother had not had me, she would still be alive"; these were my grandmother's words. I soon found myself alone even though I had a host of female influences, but I felt even more alone, open, and vulnerable without their guidance. Which then started my downward spiral of abuse and alcoholism.

I had allowed my abuser's lies and the harsh words from my grandmother to shape my opinion of myself due to my low self-esteem, anger, and resentment. Now that I am older, it's easier for me to see that people will grieve in different ways, including blame or guilt, which leads to saying things they don't mean. But at that time, it was damaging to me because I was searching for a connection; instead, I was met with resistance and denial. The situations we lived through does not have to be true for our daughter's either. We can help shape our children's future by being open and honest about our backstories and what we went through. I firmly believe that transparency is an important part of healing.

To be transparent shows that "I have a past, I have a story to tell, and I am not ashamed." Transparency is the vehicle to freedom, freedom from others' beliefs of who we should be, and freedom from our self-hatred.

The ability to be transparent is also a way to help others to be free. We never know how our story can help change someone else's path. Transparency also opens the door of communication between mothers and their children.

"When I first explained to my daughter about the relationship between her father and me, I was scared wondering what she would think of me as a woman?" So I avoided that topic; instead, I let my daughter bring the topic up on her own. She asked me, "why doesn't my dad want to see me and my brother" she was only eight at the time, so I made up an excuse as to why he was never around. I wanted to allow her to form her own opinion and have her version of him.

It wasn't until he passed my daughter came in and sat on my bed and said, "okay, mom, I need the truth" I asked her if she was sure she wanted to hear what I was about to say, and she said that she was sure. In two hours, my daughter learned about the physical abuse and the alcoholism. At the end of our talk, with tears in her eyes, she admitted she had already known about the physical abuse; she had heard us arguing one night and then remembered seeing him choking me. She just never spoke about it.

It was in that moment of transparency that we formed an even stronger bond. So many times, as mothers, we try to hide things from our children, to protect them, to shelter them. But what we may not know is they already know what we are trying to hide. Transparency is key to opening up many relationships and stronger bonds.

Journal

Chapter 10

What Is Healing?

Healing is the mental, physical, and emotional bonding of one person. When on the path to healing, it is essential we understand that just like our trauma didn't happen overnight, neither will our recovery. Healing is first conceived in the heart, which then transforms our thoughts and then transforms our actions. A child may have seen their mother working hard to love and accept others while pushing the child's love away, and the child may adopt the same trait. They long for their parents' love but are unwilling to accept the help of another supportive female figure. Dysfunction tends to breed dysfunction; it's a cycle that appears in many ways and many forms until someone is bold enough to stop the cycle. In order for the cycle to stop, someone has to be willing to admit there is a cycle that needs to be broken.

People should be aware that they have to deal with the scars they are left with. Trauma scars are like surgical scars; they are often deep cuts and can take weeks, days, months, maybe even years to heal.

Surgical scars are intentional; the cuts are used to gain access to something inside us that needs repair. "In 2017, I had started losing feeling on the left side of my body. It began with light numbness and tingling, so I wrote it off as nothing serious; as time moved on, the numbness turned into not being able to walk. I went from a cane to a walker to a wheelchair in less than a week. It was at that moment I knew something serious was happening. I went to the doctor, and it was there he told me that if I did not have the surgery, I would have approximately two weeks left to live because I was losing spinal fluid at a rapid pace.
There was something seriously wrong on the inside of me that was affecting me physically."

The doctors would need to fix the problem from the outside instead of going inside. My healing had to take place from the inside out. Trauma scars are often unintentional and tend to change the perspective of how we think and feel. The similarities are that both happen inwardly and have an effect outwardly.

The beautiful part of healing from trauma is that recovery helps change our perspective from what works to help us get better and heal. Healing teaches us about character building and strength. Overall, it provides a greater understanding of who we truly are. Healing often leads to gratitude; it takes us to a place where we are grateful for our experiences. We become grateful for healing because we can see past the hurt and know what to pay attention to in our relationships to come. We learn how to place healthy boundaries and not to accept less than what we are worth. Identifying the cycle requires being honest with ourselves and asking if I am still fighting with it? Am I still holding on to grudges? Have I let go of old hurts? Am I seeking acceptance from a toxic relationship? These are some difficult questions that we need to ask ourselves to start our road to healing. These questions also leave us open and vulnerable. But let's walk through each one.

What am I still fighting with?

Some people struggle with self-confidence; some struggle with self-worth, which causes them to be in situations where they can be taken advantage of. Many of those are words that people have called us said to us that still linger in the back of our minds. "I was in an abusive relationship for years, and he would tell me things like no matter what, I was always worthless. And for so long, I tried to show him that I'm not worthless." Once my efforts failed, it then made me afraid even to try." I could not see that he had his flaws and projected them on to me, but it took many tries to get over feelings of being worthless or unloved. Many of our wounds come from the words of those we love and trusted that had spoken to us. The words are so impressionable that we long to connect as human beings even if that situation is less than desirable. So, think about has anyone spoken a word or phrase to you that still haunts you that you still kind of feel like "maybe they were right?" If so, now is your chance to change the way you speak. When those thoughts arise, challenge yourself to talk about positivity in your life like "I am worthwhile."

Am I still Holding a Grudge?

Did you know that holding a grudge can affect you not only mentally but also physically? Holding a grudge is a path where stress and anxiety live. Think about when was the last time you saw someone who "did you wrong" how did you feel? Did your blood pressure rise? Did your jaw get tense? Those are all signs that you may be holding a grudge. Stress takes a toll on the body in various ways.

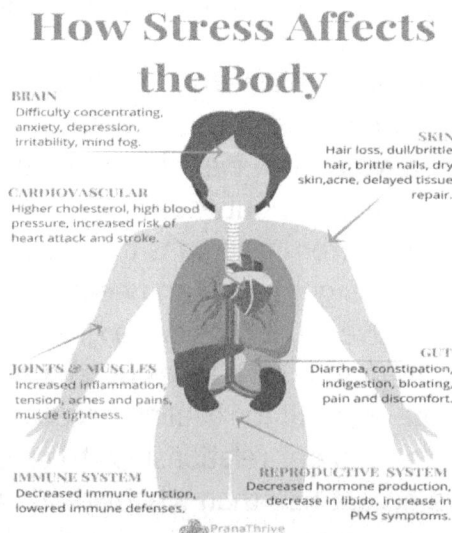

How Stress Affects the Body

BRAIN
Difficulty concentrating, anxiety, depression, irritability, mind fog.

SKIN
Hair loss, dull/brittle hair, brittle nails, dry skin, acne, delayed tissue repair.

CARDIOVASCULAR
Higher cholesterol, high blood pressure, increased risk of heart attack and stroke.

JOINTS & MUSCLES
Increased inflammation, tension, aches and pains, muscle tightness.

GUT
Diarrhea, constipation, indigestion, bloating, pain and discomfort.

IMMUNE SYSTEM
Decreased immune function, lowered immune defenses.

REPRODUCTIVE SYSTEM
Decreased hormone production, decrease in libido, increase in PMS symptoms.

PranaThrive

As we can see from the above diagram, stress takes a toll on our entire body. It is better to be able to release a grudge and work on healing yourself. Now that we know how a grudge can affect us in our minds and bodies, what do we do to overcome or let go of that grudge? How do we forgive that unfaithful partner, the unloving and absent mother? How do we get over that breach of trust? Acknowledge the hurt- your feeling is just that your feelings! You can be upset; angry you have that right. Whatever they did to hurt you was a real occurrence. To address it, you can journal or even write it out in a letter or face yourself in a mirror, pretend it's them and speak your truth. The worst thing to do would be to keep those feelings bottled up inside.

Choose to Forgive- Forgiving is for you; it's the best gift you can give yourself so that you don't have to hold a grudge. Forgiving is NOT reconciling or forgetting what happened, but it's a chance to set yourself free.

Change the narrative- you can deepen your curiosity and explore why the person needs to dwell on the past and where they are now. Why do we want to hang on to the past? Why not make changes to move forward.

Practice Letting Go- Empathy enables forgiveness. Recognizing the other person's perspective – that he or she has unresolved pain, too, or acting in their self-interest may unavoidably conflict with yours – can help you deal with your hurt. Healing is a conscious choice. We can continue to allow the trauma to continue, or we can say, "I have carried this hurt long enough; it's time for a change." And make a conscious effort to make the necessary changes.

Journal

Chapter 11
Overcoming obstacles

When we face difficult decisions in our past, we can say that there are two reactions: we can become anxious and run or stand up and fight. Obstacles that occur in everyday life and how we handle them will determine if our plans will be changed, stopped, or continue. Barriers can lead to lost time, aggravation, and frustration. However, if we take a step back and look at the obstacles we may be facing, it can also be beneficial for us as well. I know that may sound strange, but maybe there could be a piece of detail that we missed. Perhaps something was missed in our original plans, making our current obstacle bigger than it needs to be. Obstacles can show us two different things about ourselves. Obstacles will show us where we have grown in our lives, including having the conscious mind to forgive even when the person has not asked for forgiveness or if we choose to hold a grudge. Many times, we carry burdens and grudges from years, days, weeks, and months ago. Carrying around all that extra baggage does nothing for us but weighs us down. To help us understand our obstacles better, let's go over the different types of obstacles so we know how to handle them better.

External Obstacles- These obstacles are things that we cannot control, such as natural disasters—slow traffic on the way to an important meeting.
Internal Obstacles- Things we can control, issues, or circumstances due to finances, or how we interact with friends and family.
Repetitive obstacles- These are obstacles that keep recurring in our lives due to running or not facing situations head-on. When we prolog dealing with a situation, we will continue the same scenario with different people until we learn the lesson and not run from it.

Obstacles are great teachers and bookmarks to see where we need to improve our personal lives. Some of us had trauma happen at a young age doesn't go away; instead, it festers and manifest itself in many ways, and it is mainly mental, there are different ways to handle obstacles, and we will discuss that in this chapter.

Step one, get away from the drama! When we tend to run off emotion in the middle of a situation when we run off emotions, we are not thinking clearly, which means our decisions won't be rational.

Step two, assess the situation that is causing the stress of the anxiety of this obstacle. Often, we are overwhelmed by the problem that we cannot correctly determine where the situation is more intense or what area of obstacle we need to focus on.

Step three, support group or peers having a safe place where you can vent, cry and get all your frustration out is critical because the worst thing you can do is bottle up your emotions and feelings.

When we do that, it's like a volcano, and we hold all that in until our thoughts and feelings are suddenly spilling out. It's better to get things out in a safe space if you feel uncomfortable disclosing this information to a support group or a very reliable friend. Therapy is another great option; it is often looked at as an unspoken taboo, but it is a positive and safe way to express what we are experiencing; the most challenging part is facing it. Though it is tempting to run or feel like it isn't happening, the drama we experienced and happened was genuine. There are some very natural ways to help relieve the stress of feeling overwhelmed because of an obstacle we're currently facing. A healthy way that we can do that is through exercise. Science proves that exercise helps regulate heart rates, and it also enhances our moods. It's important to listen to your body! Nobody knows you like nobody else does when your body tells you when it's okay to relax, when we need to shut down the cell phone, and social media needs to go and soak in the tub and relax. Obstacles don't always have to be a form of stress. Instead, obstacles can come along to challenge physically and emotionally to grow and not to continually bring you to bring up your trauma that we endured. Obstacles can help us move forward until going on a healthier path.

Journal

Chapter 12

Setting Healthy Boundaries

Any healthy relationship in the future needs to allow us to have space to be still who we are and have personal integrity. Most people will understand and respect our boundaries when you explain our boundaries and what they mean in our lives, and how they affect us in everyday living. As we expect others to be mindful and respectful of our boundaries, we also need to be aware of other people's limits or boundaries. Because we as people are as unique as fingerprints, which means we also learn and communicate differently. We will most likely run into someone who will invade our space or cross lines, not meaning to be malicious, not to be confused with some who will want to take over their space and yours.

Suppose we are lucky enough to adapt and have a positive experience to have a trusting attitude towards others in earlier stages. In that case, others grew up with large amounts of instability, inconsistency, invasion of boundaries, and physical harm threats. Hence, they have a not so positive view of trust, which makes them more vulnerable to and open to a boundary violation.

In this chapter, we are going to go over the types of boundaries.

Verbal Boundaries: Simply put, not allowing you to speak or allowing you to be heard. These people violate your verbal boundaries by things that discount your integrity by screaming at you or gossiping about you.

Emotional Boundaries: These people attack your self-esteem. These people could also use things told in total confidence to them against you, including lying to you, making fun of you for the things you have been through, feelings you may have expressed, etc. The signs of growth of emotional boundaries are when we no longer feel the need to blame others for our problems; we can take responsibility for our actions. Strong boundaries protect us physically and emotionally. They help to protect our self-esteem as well as our identity.

Physical Boundaries: This includes taking over your personal space or unwanted touch. It may take a few interactions with other people over time before determining your boundaries and learning to respect them. Ultimately it's up to us to state our boundaries and let others know what they mean to us. If we find that someone is not respectful of our boundaries, it may indicate that we may need to reconsider having that individual part of our lives. If you are unsure if your boundaries are being pressed or crossed, here are a couple of things to look out for.

How do you feel when around that person? When people are crossing the line, we usually feel stress, anxiety, and extreme discomfort. These feelings come from feeling like we were taken advantage of, and boundary lines were crossed. Mostly in relationships, especially in the beginning, we can feel those feelings but tend to push past those "red flags" for many reasons. We feel tolerant but do not enjoy being around that person. Maybe some of us are looking for companionship and friendship. It goes back to wanting to be accepted, which connects to how we feel about ourselves. "Rihanna stated that despite her outwardly confident attitude, she still has extreme anxiety before a show." Many of us display an outward appearance of confidence but secretly, on the inside, long for acceptance.

If we continue to be around people that have been giving off "red flag" vibes, we tend to take on their attributes. We take on how they feel, it's the beginning of our attitude diminishing, and we live up to the other person's expectations.
We find ourselves unable to say "NO," so we say "yes" in times where we don't feel like it for fear of what that person may say or think. Weak boundaries are often characterized by a lack of self-identity. "growing up the only child, I was looked at as the spoiled one, and I had everything, the best birthdays, the best Christmas's, and so on. It stirred up a lot of envy from my friends and cousins, and while they were busy looking at the material things I had, no one ever knew that I still had an issue with acceptance. A large part of me only felt loved and cared for because of who my mother was. After her passing, it seemed as though I had become forgotten, which then, in turn, heightened my sense of longing for acceptance." We have to be most careful when we surrender our self-esteem to someone else; we open ourselves up to abuse, emotional, and then soon physical.

The road to recovery once we have chosen to have our identity back is a rough one; it's more like self-love rehab. During this time, we are getting back to who we are and throwing away the image that the other person forced us to be, which, on many occasions, can be scary. Anytime we choose to walk in the power that is us and our true identity, be warned that we will also endure doubt, fear, and other emotions. As we continue to grow into who we are and grow and mature into our senses, we will find that defining our boundaries and sticking to them will become more comfortable and more accessible. Overall, our boundaries are a means of support and protection for ourselves, and those around us should know and respect those boundaries.

Journal

Chapter 13

Balancing Life

Now that we have talked about our path to healing and we have learned about forgiveness. It's time we talk about having a balanced life—the definition of Balance: keeping or showing a balance; arranged in reasonable proportions. A balanced life is as essential to a healthy life as a balanced diet. It helps to keep us focused on our goals. What does a balanced and healthy life look like? And how do we maintain a balance between work, school, home, and family? In this chapter, we will discuss a balanced life and how to obtain and maintain it. The key to obtaining balance is not changing everything all at once. However, start each day with the intention to align with your goals and to take back control over your life.

"I live for a schedule! Everything for me is planned daily for weeks at a time. I do this because I know that I can and will get easily distracted. The biggest chunk of my day is spent on work; after work, I then have time blocked out for my family, and then afterward, usually, late at night, I have about 30 min for me time. The schedule is not 100% foolproof. Sometimes life happens, and times get moved around and mixed up, but it's at that time I calculate what I can compromise and what I cannot compromise."

Step one: Disconnect from the internet! I know, I know I can already hear you telling me why that is impossible. However, disconnecting from the internet gives your brain a chance to rest. It will help improve your sleep because you are not focused on the latest celebrity drama. If you can't unplug totally, try putting the phone down 3 hours at a time. If you are still craving social interaction, try socializing with friends and family in real life, not just online.

Step Two: Don't waste time. Learning to know what deserves time and learning what is non-essential. Having too much non-essential time in your day also adds to the stress and overflow of imbalance.

Step Three: Pay attention to your health: This should be at the top of your priority list! There is only one "you," so take care of yourself. Studies show that we are at our best if we are getting enough sleep, eating healthier (80/20), and get in some sort of exercise at least three times a week.

Step Four: Spend time alone- "this is, by far, my favorite step!" Unfortunately for some, this is a challenging task to accomplish, but it is vital to our living. Spending time alone can help creativity levels to do such things as writing, meditation, paint, etc., and can also help lower our stress levels.

Step Five: Pamper Yourself- Learning to take time out for yourself will be your biggest reward. Scheduling a pedicure at your local salon, schedule a massage, have a glass of your favorite wine while relaxing in a bubble bath. Your time doesn't have to be a major expense but something that helps you relax and rest. You will find that once you have figured out a schedule. Having all that you need to be sorted out, you will also notice how far less stressed you will feel. Learning to say no and learning to make time for yourself are two critical ingredients for balancing your life with healthy boundaries.

There is another aspect of balance. It's spiritual balance; having spiritual balance also helps with adding peace and foundation into your life. One of the ways I learned about spirituality was through meditation and prayer. So many times, life can get complicated, and we need answers to situations and questions. As we stated in the previous chapter, Alone time can also be part of your meditation and prayer time.

When I first started meditation, I was so skeptical about how well this would work. And as previously stated, I also get distracted easily. So, sitting for ten minutes, with my mind focused on nothing, made me doubtful, mainly because most of the time, my mind is focused on work, or my schedule, or even cooking for dinner. But I found as I sat there, I trained my mind to not focus on what is going on around me. I learned to focus on what is going on in me. I focused on how I was feeling, what was concerning me. I learned to focus on myself. When learning to meditate, it is best, to begin with, five minutes in a quiet place with no distractions. As you get the hang of meditation, you can feel free to meditate longer.

You are setting your goals or setting intentions; with this comes the realization of your dreams. This lets the Universe know you are aware of what you need and asking for assistance in achieving that goal. This also goes hand in hand with the "law of attraction" the law of attraction is I think therefore I am, or I will have. This means, in this process, to be as specific as possible. Consistency, being consistent in meditation, and setting your goals even when you feel frustrated and feel like giving up. Our journey to spiritual awakening is one that varies from person to person. We all will not arrive at awakening at the same time, nor will we all gain understanding and enlightening at the same time either. The important part is that we have taken our physical, mental and emotional health into consideration and are making strides to be completely happy. The Ultimate form of healing is the mind-body and spirit coming together as one.

Lastly, learning to ask for help. It's good to have a safe space to vent and talk with our friends; however, there may be times to ask or seek professional assistance. I know that therapy is sometimes considered something to be ashamed of or a taboo, but it is another healthy tool and outlet to express ourselves in an unbiased environment. The goal of healing is to be whole physically, mentally, and emotionally even if that means being uncomfortable while getting to know ourselves.

Journal

Chapter 14

Balancing Chakras

The body is divided into seven parts; these seven parts are called our Chakras. Whenever there is a blockage or a disconnect in our Chakras, it will adversely affect the body's area. In the chart below it will show the seven gates of the body. Each Chakra can provide healing and uplifting energy based on the energy of the affected area.

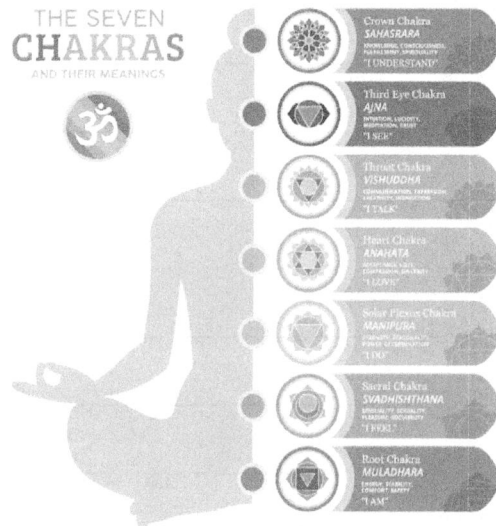

The Root Chakra - is our relationship with the earth. Its' main influence is over passion, youthfulness, and creativity.

The Sacral Chakra - this Chakra represents the water element; it impacts our joyful, happy, and compassionate side. It also affects our desires and sexuality and reproductive organs.

The Solar Plexus Chakra - is possibly the most profound and powerful Chakra; it deals mainly with our powers. It affects our professional and personal success.

The Heart Chakra - This Chakra deals with our professional and personal relationships. It is mainly associated with the air element of the body. The heart is the central part of the body; the secrets we hide in our hearts can either build up or destroy our relationships. Also, in the heart, we can decide if jealousy, envy, or lust will live, or will we fill our hearts with love, joy, and gratitude.

The Throat Chakra - Just as it sounds, the throat chakra is our inner voice. It determines our ability to be able to speak confidently. It also controls our ability to show empathy.

The Third Eye Chakra - basically, the center of our knowledge. It also affects our ability to rationalize and come to rational decisions. This Chakra happens to be also connected with the pineal gland.

The Crown Chakra - this Chakra is closely aligned with the element of light. It is associated with many organs in the body, mainly the brain, the hand, the nervous system, and the pituitary gland.

Being fully aware of the seven Chakras and their respective colors and the organs they impact will help you notice the improvements you can bring into your physical and spiritual health. Since we spoke about how they can positively enhance the body, we will also explore what happens when there is a blockage in the chakras. One thing that you will notice is that you will hear meditation mentioned a lot. Meditation is like rehab for our bodies. It's a physical and mental health review of our bodies.

One way to determine if our Chakras are out of sync or unbalanced is to check our emotions. Suppose you find that you are experiencing an abundance of anxiety, fears, nightmares. That means that somewhere there is a blockage, the best way to clear a chakra block is meditation and prayer. Some will also carry gemstones associated with the chakras to help remove them. Also, some will do a form of smudging or sage burning to clear the air. Smudging is like taking a spiritual bath. It's used to rid ourselves, our homes of negative energy and replace them with lots of joy and happiness. Many smudging methods are most commonly used by burning sage and letting the smoke cleanse our space's atmosphere. Smudging started centuries ago as part of spiritual cleaning and for the healing of the mind and body.

Each Chakra is closely aligned with its region of the body. So, if we have an overwhelming sense of depression, that would be our Sacral Chakra. If you are experiencing jealousy, envy, hatred towards individuals, the Heart chakra may be unbalanced. Having the inability to speak or vocalize your true feelings, the Throat Chakra may be blocked as well. When doing self-introspection through either meditation or by facing yourself in the mirror when we feel there is an imbalance, it is our responsibility to seek to align ourselves to achieve balance mentally, physically, and emotionally. As we can see, our path to healing helps us from the inside out. Again, the goal of healing is to reconnect the mind-body and spirit to be one.

Journal

Conclusion

My sincerest and most profound prayer is that as you read this book, it helps clarify and understand our childhood and our traumas. As you read this book, it is also my hope and prayer that you also decided to embark on your healing and spiritual awakening and balanced path. We do not have to continue to hold ourselves hostage to the hurts and pains of the past. Instead, we can trade our pain and hurt for prosperity, peace, and balance. So we can finally answer that question of Sis, who hurt you?

Citations Page

https://www.psychologytoday.com/us/articles/200111/recovering-traum

https://www.psychologytoday.com/us/articles/200111/recovering-trauma

Robert J Sternberg, Yale University. A Triangular Theory of Love. From Psychological Review,1986, Vol.93, No. 2,119-135. Found at

http://pzacad.pitzer.edu/~dmoore/psych199/1986_sternberg_trianglelove.pdf
2 Study.com: Sternberg's Triangular Theory of Love: Definition, Examples & Predictions. Found

Parnathrive.com- stress chart diagram

Handsonhealthsheffield.com- Chakra Diagram.

https://www.psychologytoday.com- mother daughter patterns.

Wellandgood.com

Made in the USA
Las Vegas, NV
28 October 2023